God is love

1 John 4:8
God shows His love for you and me
It shines so bright for the whole world to see
But do we truly know how good His love can be
No Word can describe it from A to Z
You can search the whole
dictionary and you'll agree
There's No Word in the whole world's
VOCABULARY
NO WORD

Faith, Hope and Love—
but the greatest of these is love.

And now I will show you the most excellent way. 13 If I speak in the tongues of men and of angels, but have not love, I am only a resounding gong or a clanging cymbal. 2. If I have the gift of prophecy and can fathom all mysteries and all knowledge, and if I have a faith that can move mountains, but have not love, I am nothing. 3. If I give all I possess to the poor and surrender my body to the flames, but have not love, I gain nothing. 4. Love is patient, love is kind. It does not envy, it does not boast, it is not proud. 5. It is not rude, it is not self-seeking, it is not easily angered, it keeps no record of wrongs. 6. Love does not delight in evil but rejoices with the truth. 7. It always protects, always trusts, always hopes, always preserves. 8. Love never fails. But where there are prophecies, they will cease; where there are tongues, they will be stilled; where there is knowledge, it will pass away. 9. For we know in part and we prophesy in part. 10 But when perfection comes, the imperfect disappears. 11. When I was a child, I talked like a child, I thought like a child, reasoned like a child. When I became a man, I put childish ways behind me. 12. Now we see but a poor reflection as in a mirror; then we shall see face to face. Now I know in part; then I shall know fully, even as I am fully known. 13. And now these three remain: faith, hope and love. But the greatest of these is love.

1 Corinthians 13: 1-13

Dedication

This book is dedicated to all the people of this
world. We all need God in our lives today;
Because without God, there is No-Way!

We must Believe:

If you believe, you will receive whatever you ask for in prayer.
Matthew 21:22

We must have Faith:

And without Faith it is impossible to please God,
because anyone who comes to Him must believe that He
exists and that He rewards anyone who earnestly seek Him!
Hebrews 11:6

We must have Trust:

In God, who I praise, in God I trust; I will not be
afraid. What can a mortal man do to me?
Psalm 56:4

God has Everything Under Control!

God makes our impossible, possible to do; it's
all about God, it's not about You!

*To God Be The Glory For The Things He Has Done
And Will Do!*

Christian Poems

By
Michael Ray Williams

ISBN 978-1-64028-413-5 (Paperback)
ISBN 978-1-64028-414-2 (Digital)

Christian Faith Publishing, Inc.
296 Chestnut Street
Meadville, PA 16335
www.christianfaithpublishing.com

Printed in the United States of America

Acknowledgements

Thank you Lord for giving me the talent to write poetry.
To God Be The Glory For The Things He Has Done
And Will Do!

God Doesn't Stop
People we must understand how important God is in our lives
Without Him We Are Nothing

God comes first in our lives
Always believe in the Lord our God in all things you do;
If He can do it for me;
He can do it for you

There is nothing God can't do;
Believe strongly in Him for your breakthrough!

Don't Ever Stop Believing

I would like to thank my wife, and family
for their support They're Great!

Thanks to Matt Nuce for designing my book cover,
and all my friends for also supporting me
God Bless

Table of Contents

To God Be The Glory
For The Things He Has Done

And Will Do!

Backslide

Return, faithless people;
I will cure you of backsliding.
Yes, we will come to you, for
you are the Lord our God.

Jeremiah 3:22

Backslide

Why would a person think to Backslide
Is it because their Faith has died

God says: Hebrews 13:5

Never will I leave you
Never will I forsake you

That tells the love God has for you
Our love for Him should be the same too

People face problems everyday
That's part of life they're here to stay

No matter what you're going through
Don't quit on God whatever you do

He's always there when we stumble and fall
Use His prayer line just make that call

He makes our impossible possible to do
It's all about God it's not about you

So when things get tough like they sometimes will
And we question God what's the deal

God Replies

There's nothing that I cannot do
So stay with Me I'll help you through

To Live is Christ
To Die is Gain

Choices

He is the Rock
His works are perfect,
and all His ways are just.
A faithful God who does no wrong,
upright and just is He.

Deuteronomy 32:4

Choices

We make choices everyday
24-7 some how some way

Whether we realize it or not
Some choices we make without even a thought

But the most important choice we'll ever make
Is to have God in our lives
Whatever it will take

So the choice is ours it shouldn't be a thought

No God in your life
What's your excuse for Why Not

Trust in the Lord with all your heart and lean not on
your own understanding,
In all your ways acknowledge Him and
He will make your paths straight.
(Proverbs 3:5-3:6)

How can we lose
When we choose

GOD

The Cross

Let us fix our eyes on Jesus,
the author and the perfecter of our faith,
who for the joy set before Him endured the
cross,
scorning it's shame,
and sat down at the right hand
of the throne of God

Hebrews 12:2

The Cross

A cross
The cross
That old wooden cross

Our Savior died one gloomy day
On that old wooden cross He had to stay

They showed Him no mercy on their part
The plan was to kill Him from the start

They beat Him
Spit on Him
Nailed Him to the cross for display
Then they sat around and guarded Him until
He passed away

What a way to die for an innocent man
Never hurting anyone helping everyone He can

That old wooden cross couldn't hurt anyone
But when they used it to kill
The damage was done

Jesus died on the cross that day
But He arose from the dead
And He's back to stay

Jesus Then
Jesus Now
Jesus lives Forever

The Devil

Submit yourselves, then, to God.
Resist the Devil,
And he will flee from you.

James 4:7

The Devil

The devil's a liar the devil's a cheat
There's nothing about him that is neat

He's just nasty he's no good
So please stay with God I wish you would

Don't let him have you doing wrong
Please stay with God where you belong

The devil will try all kinds of ways
If you fall into his trap it could go on for days

He really tries when you are down
So watch out for him he's all around

He likes when things go wrong for you
And you blame it on God just like most do

God's the Truth the Life and the Way
So stay with God every day

God is Good God is Great
We think He's slow but He's never late

Faith

"Have Faith in God,"
Jesus answered

Mark 11:22

Faith

Faith—The substance of things hoped for
the evidence of things not seen! (Hebrews 11:1)

God Says:

What little faith you have in Me
Yet I created all that you see

All the faith you'll really need
Is truly the size of a mustard seed

We put our faith in a brand new car
Because when we travel it will take us far

We put our faith in an ordinary chair why not
Is it going to break not even a thought

Yet when it comes to believing in God
We question Him isn't that odd

We must believe that God is for real
And what He promises us is A Done Deal

Don't Ever Stop Believing

The Flesh

For all have sinned and fall short
of the glory of God

Romans 3:23

Therefore, if anyone is in Christ,
he is a new creation;
the old has gone the new has come!

2 Corinthians 5:17

The Flesh

Our human flesh
It's a terrible mess

In and out of sin
Over and over again
(Romans 3:23)

Why does it begin
When will it end

We need Jesus Christ to help us along
Because to fight against sin
You have to be strong

Get to know Jesus
Learn from Him all that you can

Because there's no better teacher
Than The Sinless Man

Jesus Christ
Lord and Savior

God Is The Greatest

For God is the King of all the earth;
sing to Him a psalm of praise.

Psalm 47:7

God Is The Greatest

God is the Greatest this is No Doubt
So people please please listen to what I'm talking about

If you have troubles and don't know where to go
Please take it to God He tells us so

He always knows what we're talking about
And in "His Time" He will work things out

Prayer is power prayer is strong
When you pray to God you can't go wrong

God wants us all to be on His side
So get with Him and please please
Don't Backslide

This is the most important thing everyone
must know
Don't worry get to know God
He has Everything Under Control

Stay with God through Thick and Thin
You'll be greatly rewarded in the end

Heaven

Heaven

Our Father in Heaven, hallowed be your name,
your kingdom come, your will be done on earth
as it is in Heaven.
Give us today our daily bread, Forgive us our debts,
as we also have forgiven our debtors.
And lead us not into temptation,
but deliver us from the evil one.

Matthew 6:9-13

Heaven

Heaven is a place that all people should know
But Heaven is a place all people won't go

Get saved live saved welcome aboard
You've prepared yourself to be with the Lord

This world today is such a disgrace
God's Heaven and its glory is a beautiful place

Why would a person not want to go
Is it because they just don't know

Maybe satan has broken down their soul
And they're all messed up they don't care to go

Some people don't think Heaven's really around
They believe when you die you're just put in the ground

I hate to say but you're going to miss out
If you don't change your ways and
learn what God's all about

God gave us the Bible so we would know
But the choice is ours if we want to go

This temporary place doesn't even compare
To what God has promised for us up there

So come along when it's time to go
Time's getting short only God will know

Heaven or Hell
Which One Is Your Trail

17

Help

So do not fear, for I am with you;
do not be dismayed, for I am your God.
I will strengthen you and help you;
I will uphold you with My
righteous right hand.

Isaiah 41:10

Help

When you're lonely and things aren't right
God says call on Me morning noon and night

He will help you when you're down
He says just ask I'm always around

When you're having a bad day and you can't win
And the devil's tempting you with his nasty sin

Just take it to God He already knows
But He wants to hear from you about them woes

God is there to help me and you
And it's not just particular things but all that we do

He wants to help just try Him out
That's what the prayer line is all about

God says
I'm always here ready for you
And there is nothing that I can't do

God is Good God is Great
We think He's slow but He's never late

Jesus Christ

Jesus answered,
I am the Way and the Truth and the Life.
No one comes to the Father
except through Me.
If you really know Me, you would know my
Father as well.
From now on, you do know
Him and have seen Him.

John 14:6-7

Jesus Christ

Jesus walked these troubled lands
Performing miracles with His hands

People loved Him everywhere
But there was also hate in the air

They beat Him stabbed Him hung Him on the cross
What they didn't know it was a great loss

But in three days He was back again
When He died on the cross it was for the world's sin

Just like today
People just don't know
Try Jesus Christ He's the only way to go

Jesus loves you
He doesn't pick or choose
You get with Him
And you can't lose

Jesus Christ
The Light Of The World

Just Trust In Me

Trust in the Lord with all your heart and lean
not on your own understanding;
In all your ways acknowledge Him and He will
make your paths straight.

Proverbs 3:5-3:6

Just Trust In Me

People

When will you truly Just Trust In Me

What

You Don't trust what you Can't see

Life can be simple and worry free

How

It's not hard Just Trust In Me

Problems will happen to everyone

And when they do Life Is No Fun

Trust Me

Try Me

Soon you'll know

I'm not just talk

I'm All Show

I can make great things happen and you'll agree

I'm God Almighty Just Trust In Me

Left Behind

That if you confess with your mouth "Jesus
is Lord,"
and believe in your heart that
God raised Him up from the dead, you will
be saved.
For it is with your heart that you believe and
are justified,
and it is with your mouth that
you confess and are saved.

Romans 10:9-10

Left Behind

Me Left Behind
That thought doesn't even enter my mind

You're asleep in your bed and you awake to find
You're one of the people that's been left behind

Now you think it's time to pray
So you drop to your knees and start to say

Please God take me what didn't I do
I was a good person to everyone I knew

I thought for sure this wouldn't happen to me
Being good to everyone it's a guarantee

This is the problem with some people today
They think if you're good that's the only way

Get Saved
Romans 10:9-10

Put God number one and keep Him there
Everything else in this world doesn't even compare

There wouldn't be a soul not even one
If we all just do what God wants done

It could happen anytime only God will know
So don't be surprised Be Ready To Go

Don't Be Left Behind

Life

For whoever finds Me finds life and
receives favor from the Lord

Proverbs 8:35

Life

How's life treating you today
Are you happy to be alive or would you rather pass away

Life can be rough
Life can get tough

And there comes a point when you've had enough

You've tried everything but things still go wrong
You feel so weak but you're trying to be strong

Well

You've tried the Rest
Now try the Best

Jesus Christ

We all need Jesus in our lives today
We can't make it without Him

He's the Truth the Life and the Way

Jesus Christ
The Holy One

No God; Know God

God is our refuge and strength,
an ever-present help in trouble.

Psalm 46:1

No God; Know God

It would be hard for me
To really see
A life without God
I wouldn't want it to be

What a messed up world we have today
And you don't have God to guide your way

Why

"God Can Do Anything But Fail!"

Get to know God
And know Him well
Because a life without God
Is a life with Hell

No God
Know God

Only Believe

Then they asked Him,
"What must we do to do the works God requires?"
Jesus answered, "The work of God is this:
To believe in the one He has sent"

John 6:28-29

Only Believe

Two simple words yet it's hard to do
Stop making it tough
Believe God for your breakthrough

Only Believe

No matter how hard life may get
Believe in God and Don't You Quit

Only Believe

Through the good times and the bad
When you're happy or when you're sad

Only Believe

Mark 10:27

All things are possible with God

Only Believe

Mark 9:23

"If you can'?" said Jesus.
"Everything is possible for him who believes!"

Only Believe

John 11:40

Then Jesus said, "Did I tell you that if you believed,
You would see the Glory of God!"

Only Believe

Stop believing satan when he lies to you
Believe only in God
And what He says is true

Don't Ever Stop Believing

Relationships

Wives, submit to your husbands,
as is fitting to the Lord.
Husbands, love your wives and do not
be harsh with them.

Colossians 3:18-19

Relationships

What's wrong with this world today
People just don't care what they do or say

A marriage or relationship should be strong
But people anymore just can't get along

Over senseless things you argue and fight
Because both of you think that you're right

Divorces happen everyday

Why

That's Not The Godly Way

What happened to Love
What happened to Trust
What happened to Faith
Did they all turn to Lust

Romans 12:9-10

Love must be sincere. Hate what is evil;
cling to what is good.
Be devoted to one another in brotherly love.
Honor one another above yourselves.

Respect

Show proper respect to everyone;
Love the brotherhood of believers,
fear God, honor the King.

1 Peter 2:17

Respect

For all those messed up men out there
Stop treating your wife like you don't care

Show her respect and show her love
The way God shows us from Heaven above

You should be faithful to your wife
From the very start for the rest of your life

You should treat her like a queen
With honor and respect never nasty or mean

God always comes first in your life
Next comes your family and especially your wife

Love your wife with all your heart
Nothing should separate you except
"Till Death Do You Part!"

God didn't have divorce in His plan
So love her and always

Be A Faithful Man

Ephesians 5:33
However, each one of you also must love
his wife as he loves himself, and
the wife must respect her husband.

Saved

That if you confess with your mouth "Jesus
is Lord,"
and believe in your heart that God raised
Him up from
the dead, you will be saved.
For it is with your heart that you believe
and are justified, and it is with your
mouth that you confess and are saved.

Romans 10:9-10

Saved

There's a time to laugh there's a time to cry
There's a time to be born and a time to die

There comes a time when we must pass
The body's not built for hundreds of years to last

So when you die to God be right
Because if you're not it won't be a beautiful sight

There is a Hell where people go
Just read the Bible God tells us so

Get right with God and to stay you must
Build your Faith your Belief and your Trust

Get saved it's not hard to do
Confess and Believe Then Live It Too

So if you're not saved because you're still in doubt
This is real important to know

You'll go straight to Hell and you won't get out
And Hell's not a Heavenly place to go

Burning Up

Sin

For sin shall not be your master,
because you are not under
law, but under grace.

Romans 6:14

Sin

When God created this beautiful land
He truly didn't have sin in His plan

The beautiful world that He built so well
When He created man it went to Hell

All God asked was don't eat from the tree
But when they disobeyed it started sin for you and me

Sin: The breaking of religious law or law of God.
To do something which is morally wrong

Lying stealing spouses cheating on each other
Sin is so bad a son kills his own mother

Why does the world have to be this way
Why doesn't everybody follow God's word today

Here's what I suggest for you
Some important tips that you should do

Attend church (regularly)
Find a good Bible study group
Read the Bible daily
Pray (communication with God)

To battle against sin there's no other way
But to be truly committed to God everyday

The battle is not ours
It's the Lord's

Don't Ever Stop Believing

Stress: What A Mess

The best remedy that I can find
Is God's powerful scriptures for the mind

Stress: What A Mess

When your life is a terrible mess
And you have all kinds of horrible stress

The best remedy that I can find
Is God's powerful scriptures for the mind

They will help you throughout the day
Take ALL of that horrible stress away

Watch what you Eat
Watch how you Rest
Follow God's Word
He knows what's Best

Just remember when stress is taking control
And your mind and your body's feeling really low

Some pills and rest may temporarily take it away
But without God's word it may be back that same day

God's Word Is Healing For The Soul

Success

And the Lord was with him,
he was successful in whatever he undertook.

2 Kings 18:7

Success

Success is hard work but don't you Quit
You have God in your corner and don't you Forget

He's always there to help us out
So always Believe and don't ever Doubt

Delight ourselves in the Lord (Psalm 37:4)
And He'll give us the desires of our heart
But we also have to do our part

Whatever It Takes To Succeed

We are more that conquerors in all
that we do (Romans 8:37)
When we have God's power to help us through

Tell Yourself

I can do everything through Christ who
strengthens me (Phil 4: 13)

That's good to know
Don't you agree

Now things may happen most likely they will
Just tell yourself It's No Big Deal

With God in our corner how can we fail
We just do our part and God will bless us well

Don't Ever Give Up
Believe You Can Achieve

43

Time

For it is time for judgment to begin
with the family of God;
and if it begins with us,
what will the outcome be for those who
do not obey the gospel of God?
And if it is hard for the righteous to be saved
what will become of the
ungodly and the sinner?

1 Peter 4:17-18

Time

Be smart
Don't wait until it's too late

Have you ever wondered where time goes
Could it be like the wind nobody really knows

Does time seem to go faster as we get old
Or is that just something that we are told

Tick Tock says the clock time doesn't wait
Please get yourself saved before it's too late

When today is gone it's tomorrow's past
How much time do we have how long will time last

Heaven or Hell it's up to you
The choice is yours between the two

Don't procrastinate another day
Turn your life over to God it's the only way

Respect and obey God
This is what life is all about

If you're not saved
(Romans 10: 9-10)
Do It
Before Your Time Runs Out

Who's Jesus Christ

Jesus said,
I am the Light of the World.
Whoever follows Me will never walk in
darkness,
but will have the light of life.

John 8:12

Who's Jesus Christ

Jesus Christ is the Master of all that we see
And if you know who Jesus is I'm sure you will agree

He's the Teacher the Head of the Church and Messiah too
He's everything positive for me and for you

He's a Wonderful Counselor the King of Kings
Only Begotten Son
He is the Brightest Morning Star the Prince of Peace
And The Holy One

He's The Almighty The Savior The Everlasting Father
He's The Bread of Life Alpha and Omega
And also The Living Water

Jesus Christ is a lot of things in our lives today
But just remember the most important things

He's the Truth the Life and the Way

Why Worry

Therefore I tell you,
do not worry about your life,
what you will eat or drink,
or about your body,
what you will wear.
Is not life more important than food,
and the body more important than clothes?

Matthew 6:25

Why Worry

Worry Worry Worry me
Things just aren't right why can't they be

God will take care of you

When you have a child that's really bad
And the things they do just make you mad

God will take care of you

Bills Bills Bills something always goes wrong
And your barely making it just struggling along

God will take care of you

When your marriage is completely out of control
What do you do where do you go

God will take care of you

When you go to church and try to do right
But some days are Hell from morning till night

God will take care of you

God says—Don't worry give all your problems to Me
I'll take care of you just trust Me you'll see

STOP WORRYING

Matt 6:25-34 or Luke 12:22-31

Will You Marry Me

Marry Jesus with all your heart
Nothing will separate you
Not Even Death Do You Part

Will You Marry Me

And now I pronounce you husband and wife
Forever and ever for the rest of your life

Hi
My name is Jesus

Will you marry Me
I'll treat you better than anyone you see

I'm not into looks money or fancy cars
I'll marry you just the way you are

I'm not prejudice in any way
I'll love you no matter what you do or say

Men women and little kids too
I will marry everyone of you

I'm looking to serve as a good husband or wife
To be faithful to you even after this life

So marry Me
Stay with Me and you'll see
We'll be together
For
Eternity

Jesus Christ
Author and Finisher of our Faith

50 Years Strong

Honor and Cherish your Marriage

This poem 50 Years Strong is a very
special poem

I wrote it for my in-laws on
their 50th anniversary

50 Years very unusual now days

People just don't treasure
God's vows anymore

Marriage is the hardest job
a person will ever face

And people walk out continuously
That's Such A Disgrace

God didn't intend for us to separate

Stay together with Love

Not divide with Hate

50 Years Strong

50 years—That's a pretty big task
What's your secret may I ask

Tell the world what you have found
Because there's too many divorced people around

I bet it's Love
True love so strong
Because with it you can't go wrong

Or maybe it's Trust
Someone you can depend on
Without the confidence or faith
Your marriage is gone

Marriage should be "Till Death Do You Part"
All God's vows you should treasure with all your heart

Whatever it was it worked for you
I wish more married couples can also
Reach 50 Plus Too.

In Closing

Always
Believe God for what He says
is True
He's always there ready to help
me and you
It doesn't matter what we're going
through
There's Nothing That Our Father
God Can't Do
God is Good all the time
And
All the time God is Good

**May God Bless
Everyone**

About the Author

Michael Williams was born in a small town called Salina, located in the Sun Flower State of Kansas. He is 2nd youngest of five siblings, two boys and three girls. It was in 2003 when Michael received his calling to minister through poetry. Completing his first book *To God Be The Glory vol.1*, Michael actively ministered his publication in Kansas, at the local Churches.

In 2003 his oldest daughter, Season, relocated to Dallas, Texas faithfully following her husband, Pastor Derek Jacobs calling to ministry. It wasn't long after that Michael, his wife Michelle and 2 younger daughters soon followed. It was in Dallas that Michael Williams then faithfully completed the second of the two books, *To God Be The Glory vol. 2.*

Simple and precise poetry written so that all can easily get the message. "It has to be simple, because I want all readers both young and old to enjoy and understand God's word", explains the author Michael Williams. Whether it's the word or Michael's passion behind his delivery, that engages and moves anyone that attends his events.

"I was moved to tears when I heard Michael's poetry, it was just what I needed to hear and when I needed to hear it", exclaimed Ms. Green a Dallas teacher that attended one of Michael's events here in Dallas. She continued "I purchased one for each of my friends and my teen daughter, I knew she needed to hear *The Answer.*"

CPSIA information can be obtained
at www.ICGtesting.com
Printed in the USA
BVHW040600200223
658834BV00002B/356